COLLIN

KEEPING Creepy Crawlies

A PRACTICAL GUIDE TO CARING FOR UNUSUAL PETS

DAVE CLARKE

First published in 2000 by
HarperCollins*Publishers*
77-85 Fulham Palace Road
Hammersmith
London W6 8JB

Collins is a registered trademark of
HarperCollins*Publishers* Limited

The HarperCollins website address is
www.**fire**and**water**.com

06 05 04 03 02 01 00
9 8 7 6 5 4 3 2 1

Text and design © HarperCollins*Publishers* Ltd, 2000
Photographs © David Manning, 2000
Illustrations © Felicity Rose Cole, 2000

**A catalogue record of this book is available from the
British Library**

Editor: Isobel Smales
Designer: Colin Brown
Photography: Animal Ark, London
Illustrations: Felicity Rose Cole

ISBN 0 00 413398 6

Colour reproduction by Colourscan, Singapore
Printed and bound by Printing Express Ltd, Hong Kong

Please Note
While every reasonable care was taken in the compilation of
this publication, the Publisher and Author cannot accept
liability for any loss, damage, injury or death resulting from
the keeping of creepy crawlies by user(s) of this publication,
or from the use of any materials, equipment, methods or
information recommended in this publication or from any
errors or omissions that may be found in the text of this
publication or that may occur at a future date, except as
expressly provided by law.

Contents

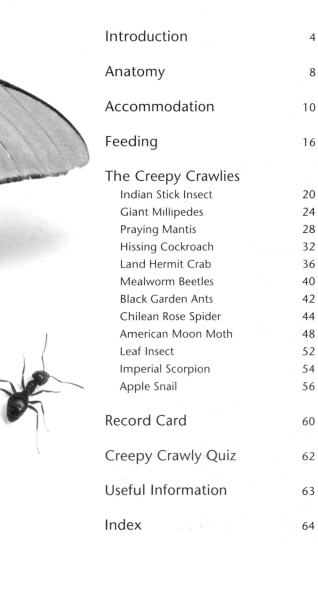

Introduction

This book is intended as a simple guide to keeping some easily available invertebrate or creepy crawly animals as pets. Invertebrates will take up very little space and most are easily cared for, which makes them ideal first pets for anyone wanting experience in looking after unusual animals at home. With the right accommodation, food and care they will make excellent pets. This book will help you to learn much more about this fascinating group of animals.

Invertebrates, animals without backbones, are often called creepy crawlies, which makes them all sound pretty nasty. People tend to be unsure about animals which are very different from humans, but that is what makes them so interesting. You will find that the animals in this book are much more wonderful and amazing than your average household pet.

Creepy crawlies can be ideal animals to keep at home. You will, however, need some specialist information to make sure that they get the right care, and that is what this book is all about. No pet should be brought home without finding out in advance what is required to keep it properly.

Invertebrate pets like this Mealworm Beetle can be very easy to keep.

Details for looking after a range of creepy crawlies are given here, with information on the main types of accommodation grouped for species in four main categories – arboreal (tree-living), terrestrial (ground-living), underground, and aquatic (living in water). Then there are details on food and feeding, whether the creepy crawlies are vegetarians (plant-eating), insectivores (insect-eating) or omnivores (eat both plant and animal material). The main part of the book covers in detail 12 different types of creepy crawly. They are arranged with the easiest to keep species at the beginning, graduating to those that are more difficult. Each species has a key to show you at a glance what kind of accommodation that species requires, what kind of diet it needs, how long it could live for and how large it may grow. Alongside the keeping information there are suggested observation points for studying your pets. A quiz will then test your knowledge of creepy crawlies. The creepy crawlies in this book can be acquired from pet shops, specialist invertebrate suppliers, or from entomological (insect) shows. With care

The American Moon Moth is a bit more of a challenge to rear.

they can be kept very successfully and even bred at home. Most can be picked up and held in the hand, but they must be handled with care. They are often delicate and easily damaged, and should not be disturbed too often, certainly not more than once a day. Animals like spiders and scorpions that can bite or sting are better left alone.

Hermit crabs can live for a very long time if properly cared for.

Often people think creepy crawlies are a nuisance and are not very valuable. Although there are a few species that are pests, the majority do not cause any damage and avoid contact with people. In fact most of them are extremely beneficial, and have a vital role to play in pollinating flowers or recycling food that other animals do not eat. Insects like bees are essential for pollinating fruit crops, and millipedes are one of the best recyclers of decaying plant matter, putting the goodness back into the soil for plants and ultimately other animals to use. Without this important work, all life on earth could not survive. It is important that everyone appreciates the role that all animals play. Invertebrates are a major element of biodiversity – the variety of life. Many of them are now threatened, and need protection in the wild or captive breeding. Conservation organisations like zoos are working hard to protect species and educate about the wonder of nature. It is only when people see how amazing invertebrates are close up that they realize how incredible they are. Your pets can also do their bit to help change other people's attitudes to creepy crawlies. So next time someone says something nasty about a creepy crawly, you can put them right. And then, why not introduce them to your pet?

KEY

Alongside the main information for each species, there is a simple key to show at a glance what the keeping requirements are for each creepy crawly.

Accommodation

Four types are necessary. Arboreal for tree-living species, terrestrial for ground dwellers, underground for burrowers and aquatic for those living in water.

Diet

Three types of diet must be catered for. Plant-eating vegetarians, insect-eating insectivores, or omnivores which eat both plant and animal material.

Maximum Life Span

Life expectancy varies from several months up to over 10 years. Remember, you must be prepared to look after your pet throughout its life.

Maximum Length

Some creepy crawlies are only a few millimetres long (less than 0.1in), whilst the largest invertebrate in this book can reach over 15cm (6in).

Delicate baby Leaf Insects need extra special care and attention.

Anatomy

Unlike humans and other vertebrate animals, creepy crawlies (invertebrates) do not have an internal skeleton. The animals in this book are all members of two huge groups of invertebrates, arthropods and molluscs.

Arthropods

Most creepy crawlies are arthropods, animals with an external skeleton and jointed limbs. Arthropods have to regularly shed their external skeleton or exoskeleton as they grow, which is called ecdysis or moulting. The difference in size and shape after each moult can be quite dramatic.

Insects

Ants, moths, beetles, cockroaches, stick insects and mantids are all insects. Insects have 3 parts to their bodies; the head, thorax and abdomen. The eyes and mouth are at the front of the head, which also has a pair of sensory feelers called antennae. All insects have 3 pairs of legs, connected to the thorax.

The abdomen stores food. Insects undergo metamorphosis (a complete change of shape) as they grow, and the young (called a larva or nymph) and adult insects can look very different from each other. Many insects go through an immobile nonfeeding stage of development between larva and adult, called a pupa, and sometimes the pupa is protected by a silky cocoon.

Antennae

Eyes

Head

Wings – only the fore-wings are visible

Thorax

3 pairs of legs

Segmented abdomen

Millipedes

Like insects, millipedes have antennae, but the elongated body has lots of segments, each carrying 2 pairs of legs.

Spiders and scorpions

Spiders and scorpions are arachnids. They lack antennae, have 2 main parts to the body and 4 pairs of legs. They have a pair of extra limbs at the front of the body called pedipalps, which look like smaller legs in spiders, but these form the claws in a scorpion.

Eyes – spiders can have up to 4 pairs of eyes

Spinnerets for producing silk

Abdomen

4 pairs of legs

dipalps

Cephalothorax (equivalent to the head and thorax in an insect)

Crabs

Crabs are a type of crustacean, along with lobsters and shrimps. They breathe using gills. Most crustaceans are aquatic, and many of these have exposed gills. Crabs tend to hide their gills under their tail flap,

and hermit crabs have their gills hidden inside their shell.

Molluscs

A huge group of animals that includes mussels, snails and octopus. Most molluscs produce a shell to protect the soft parts of their bodies.

Snails

Snails have a soft body permanently attached to a hard shell, which grows as the animal gets bigger, usually in a coiled shape. The body has a head region with 2 pairs of sensory tentacles at the front. There is a breathing hole at the side of the body, which in aquatic snails has a long tube to reach the surface of the water. Snails move around on the flattened foot, aided by the slime that they produce.

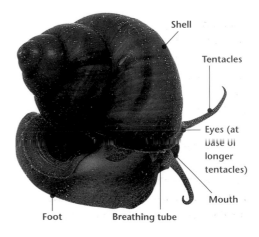

Shell

Tentacles

Eyes (at base of longer tentacles)

Mouth

Foot

Breathing tube

Accommodation

It is important to create the right environment for creepy crawlies, to keep them happy and healthy. Some species need very little specialist equipment, and a simple container without heating will be enough. However, others, particularly those from more tropical environments, require properly designed accommodation. Luckily in recent years a large amount of suitable equipment has been made available, mainly as a result of the increased popularity of keeping reptiles.

Containers

Most species can be kept in a plastic or glass tank with a well-fitting lid to prevent the animals from escaping. The best type are the readily available clear plastic containers with tight fitting vented lids, with a smaller door in the top.

The size of the containers will depend on the species but approximately 30cm (12in) in length by 20cm (8in) wide and 20cm (8in) high (shown as 30 x 20 x 20cm (12 x 8 x 8in)) is suitable for one or two individuals of most of the species discussed in this book.

The container should be positioned in a place that is safe for the animals – on a

Often called 'pen-pal' type containers, these plastic boxes are ideal for a lot of invertebrates. They also have well-fitting lids to prevent pets from escaping.

sturdy shelf, away from too much disturbance, and not near a radiator or window, where the container could become too hot or too cold.

Heating

Some species will be happy at room temperature, around 16-18°C (62-65°F).

Tropical species should be kept at around 25°C (77°F). This means they will need additional heating. The best form of heating is a heat mat, which can be positioned at the side of the tank. Ideally you should connect any form of heater to a thermostat on which you can set the required temperature. The thermostat will have a mains lead, a lead to connect it to the heater, and a sensor to monitor the temperature which needs to be positioned inside the tank. Special water heaters can be used for aquatic containers, and these usually have a built-in thermostat. Any electrical equipment must be set up carefully, so always get an adult to wire up heating equipment.

It is important to measure the temperature with a thermometer to check it is correct. The best type of thermometer has a reading for the minimum and maximum temperatures, with a probe that can be positioned where the animals are inside the tank.

Humidity

Most species, particularly those from the tropics, need a damp atmosphere to keep them healthy. A high humidity, of 70-80%, can be provided by keeping the material at the bottom of the container damp, or by regular misting. Use a hygrometer to check levels.

Hygrometer

A new, clean hand sprayer as used for house plants is ideal for damping down containers to create humidity and for providing drinking water, particularly for arboreal species.

Other equipment

Lighting

You may want to set up a light to be able to see your animals better. A fluorescent light is best, as it does not produce too much heat. Again, make sure this is wired up safely. Remember that several species are nocturnal so will hide away from bright light.

Heater pad

Thermostat

| Lighting options | Hide | Plastic plant | Cork bark |

Water filters

Aquatic species should have a water filter to help keep the container clean and to put more oxygen into the water. The easiest type to use is a small internal power filter, a single unit which has a pump head and a cleanable filter section. This is placed inside the tank underwater, usually attached with suckers. Alternatively an air pump can be used next to the tank, connected by a length of tubing to an air-powered underwater filter such as a foam filter or box filter. Ask your local aquarium shop what they recommend.

Tank furnishing

Extra items may be added to the tanks to provide shelter, climbing space or purely for decoration. Arboreal species need branches to climb. Terrestrial species can be given pieces of wood, bark or rocks. Live plants can also be used, but may be eaten or damaged by some species. Avoid using very poisonous types or spiky plants like cactus, on which the invertebrates could harm themselves. Plastic plants can be used in terrestrial or aquatic set-ups, particularly where the animals would otherwise eat the live plants.

Maintenance

All the animals in this book should be checked daily to see that they are healthy. Some species need regular cleaning but others should be left for longer. Generally vegetarians need more regular maintenance than predators, but they are easier to provide food for. When the tanks are cleaned the animals should be put in a temporary container, the paper towel or substrate removed and thrown away (looking carefully for any eggs or babies), and the plastic or glass tank and lid cleaned using a mild detergent or Milton fluid. Rock and wood decorations can also be cleaned. Make sure they are all rinsed thoroughly before setting the tank up again with fresh materials.

The animals in this book require 4 different types of accommodation, based on the habitat they are found in – arboreal, terrestrial, underground and aquatic.

Arboreal

Animals that climb need an upright container, so placing a rectangular tank on its end gives more height. Having the removable lid on the side makes changing cage decorations easier. Some paper towels or kitchen roll, placed over the base of the container, can be kept damp to maintain humidity and make it easy to clean out. Cut plants, put in as food or as dry branches, provide support for climbing.

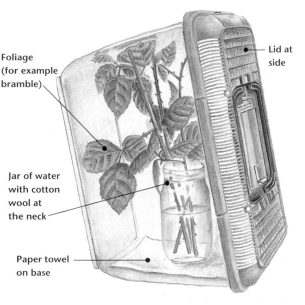

Foliage (for example bramble)

Lid at side

Jar of water with cotton wool at the neck

Paper towel on base

Pen-pal type container, upright for arboreal set-up.

Water for drinking can be provided by regular mist spraying. The container should be sprayed at least twice a day, and the animals will take water from the leaves and branches.

The container can be cleaned out whenever the foliage needs replacing.

Another type of arboreal container is the hanging net, which is mainly used for adult moths. This consists of 2 metal hoops with fine cotton or nylon mesh stretched between them, usually with a zip at the side for a door. These can be purchased from insect suppliers. One version of hanging net has an opening at the bottom where the mesh can be gathered around a jar of foliage or a growing plant, which could also be useful for keeping moth larvae or stick insects.

Terrestrial

Ground-living species need a container with the lid uppermost, for easy access. The container should have a layer of material on the bottom, the substrate, for the animals to live on. In most cases this is a layer of soil or peat (coconut fibre is a good substitute for real peat), kept damp to maintain humidity. Make sure it does not get too wet. An extra layer of gravel at the very bottom, about 1cm (0.5in) deep, will provide extra drainage. Normally a depth of 5-10cm (2-4in) of substrate is enough, to allow the animals to do some digging. The choice of material for the substrate should be right for the animal.

A water bowl can be positioned in one corner of the tank. This can be filled with cotton wool or sponge, to prevent small animals drowning in it. Some pieces of wood should be added to give hiding places. Cork bark is ideal and looks good.

The substrate in terrestrial containers can be left in for a while before it needs changing. Replace it if any fungus starts appearing, or if it becomes too wet or compacted. Spray as necessary to keep it just damp, and top up the water bowl. Food items such as vegetables should be replaced every few days to stop them going mouldy. Insectivorous species should have any uneaten food removed with a pair of long tweezers.

Underground

To easily see animals which live under the surface of the soil, a special kind of container is needed. For example, the best way to keep ants is to use an enclosure called a formicarium, an upright framework holding two pieces of glass or clear plastic with a small gap in between, filled with soil or sand. The gap only needs to be about 5mm (0.2in) for small species of ants. An open area at the top leaves room for water and food to be added. The ants can make their tunnels in the soil, and can be seen from the side. Formicaria can be purchased from specialist suppliers, or one could even be made at home.

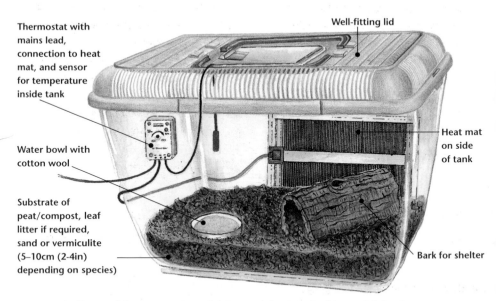

Thermostat with mains lead, connection to heat mat, and sensor for temperature inside tank

Well-fitting lid

Heat mat on side of tank

Water bowl with cotton wool

Substrate of peat/compost, leaf litter if required, sand or vermiculite (5–10cm (2-4in) depending on species)

Bark for shelter

Pen-pal type container, horizontal for tropical terrestrial set-up.

Access hole with cover

Ventilation – very fine mesh

5cm (2in) gap at top for adding food

Two small bowls, one for water and other for sugar solution

Soil mix (with burrows)

Formicarium-type container, upright, for underground set-up.

Stand for stability

Aquatic

A good waterproof container is necessary for aquatic species, and rigid plastic containers or glass aquariums like those used for tropical fish are ideal. The lid of the tank can be plastic mesh, sliding glass, or a proper aquarium-style lid which will accept a light fitting. The bottom can be covered with washed aquarium gravel. A filter will be needed, both to help keep the water clean and put more oxygen into the water. Aquatic species will need regular water changes, even if a filter is used. It is best to replace 10% of the water once a week, rather than changing a large amount of water at once. The filter will also need cleaning out regularly.

Mains leads from filter and heater

Sliding glass lid

Internal filter

Underwater heater/thermostat attached to back wall with suckers

Water level

Plastic plants

All glass aquarium for aquatic set-up.

Gravel substrate

Feeding

Invertebrate animals feed on a wide variety of foods, but the animals in this book can be placed in 3 main categories – vegetarians (which feed mainly on plant material), insectivores (which feed mainly on insects) and omnivores (which feed on both animal and plant material).

Vegetarians

Some vegetarian species eat the fresh green leaves of plants, others only eat dead or decaying leaves, and some feed on vegetables and fruit.

Green leaf-eating species must have very fresh leaves. The best way of providing these is to cut small branches or twigs carrying healthy leaves, with the cut ends placed in a jar of water. Remove any leaves that may end up underwater, and plug the opening of the jar with cotton wool to prevent the animals from drowning. You could also use a glass or plastic screw-top container with holes in the top for the stems to stick through. For most species it is important to have leaves touching the top of the tank, so they always find food. Make sure that you only collect clean leaves, not those sprayed with chemicals like insecticide. The type of leaves to collect for food depends upon the pet you are keeping, as most invertebrates only eat certain types of plants. See the individual species information for the preferred plants, and make sure the correct types are offered.

Some invertebrates prefer to eat dead or decaying leaves. Many types of naturally fallen leaves can be collected in the autumn, and stored for use throughout the year, or partly rotted leaves from a compost heap can be used.

Leaves offered as food must be clean and fresh, and be of a suitable type for the creepy crawly to eat.

Animals that eat vegetables and fruit can be fed a variety of foods that we would eat ourselves. Vegetables should be given raw. Slice open both fruit and vegetables so that it is easier for the animals to get to the softer parts. Place them on the substrate in the tank, or on a shallow dish to make cleaning easier.

Most vegetarian species, particularly caterpillars, should have access to high quality food at all times. Make sure it is renewed regularly. Be careful when removing old food that all the animals are moved from it – some, particularly eggs and babies, can be very difficult to see and may be discarded by mistake.

Insectivores

Most insectivores will only take their food live. Insects have to be bought from a pet shop or ordered by post from a breeder. The main live foods to use are crickets and locusts. Very small insectivores like baby mantids or spiders will need newly hatched crickets or small flies like fruit flies. When purchased, these will normally be supplied in tubs of many individuals which can usually be kept for a while in the container they arrive in, as long as they are fed.

Crickets can be fed on bits of vegetables, and locusts will eat grass.

Insectivores do not like food to be crawling around in their tank all the time. They should be offered one or two insects to eat, and any uneaten food should be removed after 24 hours. Food items that are left in can be irritating to your pet, and could harm them, particularly when they are moulting. The frequency of feeding depends on the age of the animal – young invertebrates need feeding more often than adults. Generally adults should be offered food about once a week. Never give them insects that are more than half their own size. You will soon be able to recognise if they are hungry by their reaction when the food goes in. Some insectivores can go for very long periods without food – the bigger spiders can last several months after a good feed.

Omnivores

Omnivores are usually scavengers, which feed on plant material and dead animals. The omnivorous animals in this book can be fed vegetables and fruit, plus bodies of dead insects or dog or cat food for protein.

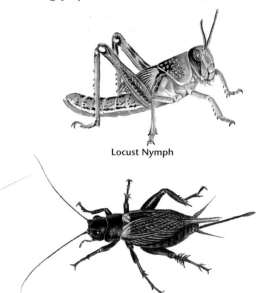

Locust Nymph

Black Field Cricket

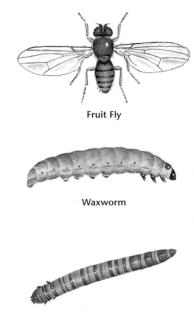

Fruit Fly

Waxworm

Mealworm

A variety of insects is available for use as live food for your pets.

(Illustrations not drawn to scale)

Fresh fruit and vegetables are suitable foods for an omnivore, but supplements are also beneficial.

Supplement foods

Fish flake or pellet foods
The foods available for aquarium fish can make a good supplement, particularly for omnivorous animals. They are high in protein and have added vitamins and minerals. They must be kept dry or they will quickly go mouldy. Offer flaked or pellet food in a shallow dish and replace this regularly.

Honey or sugar water
Many animals feed on nectar from flowers, or the sap from plant stems. Ants also collect a sugary solution from aphid insects called honeydew. To replace this they can be given diluted honey, or sugar solution of one part ordinary sugar to ten parts water, soaked in some cotton wool.

Calcium
Most invertebrates need calcium for healthy growth. Leaf-eating species get enough from the plants they eat, but other vegetarians and omnivores can be given bits of cuttlefish bone (as supplied in pet shops for birds) in their container. This should last a long time, and only needs replacing if it is all eaten or starts to go off. Insectivorous species will not eat calcium, but cuttlefish can be fed to their food insects before use.

Dried cuttlefish bones like these are a perfect way of supplying your pet with extra calcium.

Indian Stick Insect

Carausius morosus

Arboreal

Vegetarian

1 year

10cm (4in)

Stick insects can vary from only a few centimetres (1in) to 30cm (12in) body length – the longest insects in the world. But they all share the same ability to become virtually invisible amongst branches of shrubs or trees. This superb camouflage is normally their only defence against predators, although some species have spines on their legs or bodies to deter attackers. True to their name, they have thin, stick-like bodies and spend most of the day resting very still amongst plants. They become more active at night. Most stick insects are shades of brown or green, to help their camouflage, but some have brighter colours hidden away which they can 'flash' if disturbed, to put off predators. Indian Stick Insects are normally green, but some can be brown as well. They have a red patch inside their front legs, close to the body.

Indian Stick Insects can be acquired as eggs, nymphs or

Stick insects have good camouflage to protect themselves against predators.

True to their name, stick insects can be difficult to see on branches.

Fresh leaves of privet are the main diet of Indian Stick Insects.

Several stick insects of the same size can be kept together in one container.

Indian Stick Insects are some of the easiest creepy crawlies to keep in captivity.

adults. As they breed very easily, it is usually not difficult to find someone who has some to give away. If you have not kept them before, it is best to get some larger nymphs or adults, as they are more delicate when very young. They live for less than a year.

Stick insects should be kept in arboreal accommodation. A container about 30 x 20 x 20cm (12 x 8 x 8in) will be adequate for a group of up to 10 adults. Leaves provided for food should be sprayed a couple of times a day, to give the insects drinking water. The bottom of the container can be covered in tissue or paper towelling, or a small amount of soil. Indian Stick Insects do not need heating, as long as they are kept indoors in a warm room. Larger tropical stick insects can be kept in basically the same way, but in bigger containers to give them enough room to shed their skins. They will need heating, such as a heat mat on the side of the

SIMILAR SPECIES

Prickly Stick Insect
Extatasoma tiaratum

•

Spiny Stick Insect
Eurycantha calcarata

•

Fern Stick Insect
Oreophoetes peruanus

container, and a deeper damp base to the container like peat will help to keep up a higher humidity.

The Indian Stick Insect's favourite food is usually privet, but they will also eat ivy and bramble (blackberry). Some tropical types eat other plants, like oak or even ferns, but most feed on bramble leaves.

a branch moving in the wind.

Stick insects are parthenogenetic – eggs can develop without being fertilised, so males are not needed for breeding. As long as you have adult stick insects, they produce eggs that can hatch. Virtually all Indian Stick Insects are females. Males do occur, but they are very rare – less than

Indian Stick Insects are usually green, although some can be brown as well. They have red patches on the inside of the front legs.

Stick insects may be handled, but they can be quite delicate and you must be careful that they are not damaged. They should be carefully lifted off the leaves or made to walk onto a hand. Their feet have claws on the end to help them hold on, and they can be difficult to remove from fluffy clothing. They will often play dead when disturbed, holding the legs stiff against the side of the body. After a short while they will become active again, and tend to move with a wobbly motion, like

The eggs of stick insects can be very difficult to spot. They look like tiny seeds. They are smooth and rounded with a lighter coloured cap on the end.

Observation Point

Diet

In the wild, stick insects choose which plants to live on. In captivity they can only eat what we offer them. Stick insects can quite happily feed on one type of plant throughout their lives, but you can try them with different types to see what they prefer.

Put some fresh leaves of the 3 main types of food plant, privet, ivy and bramble, in the same container. The stick insects mainly feed at night, so the next day see how much of each type of plant has been eaten. You could also make a note of which parts of the plant your pets prefer. Some stick insects prefer the older leaves, while others eat the new growth. Do young stick insects and adults eat different parts?

one in a thousand is male. An adult male is smaller and skinnier than a female. In other species males are much more common, and they often have fully formed wings and use them to fly around looking for females. Indian Stick Insect eggs are only 2-3mm (0.08-0.12in) long, and look like little seeds, dropped on the ground. They are smooth and rounded in shape, dark grey with a lighter coloured cap on the end. Be careful to look for them on the base of the container. The eggs can be collected up to hatch separately. The baby stick insects will emerge about 1 month after the eggs are laid, although the time taken to hatch varies with the temperature. It is amazing how big the newly hatched insect is, compared to the size of the tiny egg. They can be kept just like the adults, but it is more important to make sure they have fresh leaves and regular misting with water. Different sizes of stick insect can be kept together, but if they run out of food, the larger ones may nibble the smaller ones, so to be safe it is best to keep them separately. Stick insects are kept by many people and it is often possible to get in touch with breeders in the amateur insect societies to swap eggs of different species. They are a good introduction to keeping and enjoying invertebrates at home.

Giant Millipede

Epibolus species

Terrestrial

Vegetarian

2-3 years

15cm (6in)

Millipedes are very important animals which recycle plant matter back into the soil. There are over 13,000 types of millipede, ranging in size from less than 1cm to 28cm (less than 0.5in to 11in). Smaller millipedes are found throughout the world, but the Giant Millipedes are only found in warmer parts, such as tropical forests. It can be difficult to identify millipedes as there are so many types and they look very similar. The Mombassan Train Millipede *Epibolus pulchripes* is easy to breed so is often available. All millipedes have segments along the body, each one carrying 2 pairs of legs, with a pair of antennae at the front. Their relatives the centipedes, which are predators, have only 1 pair of legs per body segment. Millipedes will often coil up when disturbed.

The long, bendy body of some Giant Millipedes can be up to 28cm (11in) long.

Millipedes have many legs, around 250-300 in most species.

Giant Millipedes like this one make fascinating, unusual pets and are relatively easy to keep at home.

East African Giant Millipede
Graphidostreptus species

•

Madagascar Fire Millipede
Aphistogoniulus species

•

Florida Millipede
Chicobolus spinigerus

Millipedes will coil their
body up to defend
themselves against attack.

The active antennae
on the millipede's
head are important
sense organs.

Giant Millipedes can usually be purchased as adults. Look for pairs so you can breed them. If you are not sure of their sexes, get 3 or 4 of the same type and there is a good chance you will have both sexes. Some types can live for 5 years, although the Mombassans normally live about 2-3 years.

A terrestrial container is ideal for millipedes. If they can reach the top they will try to escape, so a tight fitting lid is needed. A heat mat should be set up to provide warmth. Cover the bottom with 5-10cm (2-4in) of peaty soil, then a layer of leaf litter. Fallen oak leaves are ideal, or try sycamore, ash or beech leaves. A couple of bits of bark or moss will provide them with hiding places. They can also be given pieces of fruit and vegetables to eat, such as banana, apple, cucumber and lettuce. The fruit and vegetables should be placed directly on the substrate (so that even baby millipedes can reach them) and carefully changed every few days. Only add more leaves as they get eaten, and the soil should only be replaced if it has all been used up and turned to droppings. The container should be sprayed occasionally, to keep the soil damp but not wet. Several millipedes may be kept together, even of different species.

Giant Millipedes are great fun to handle, as long as you are careful. They will walk onto your hand, gripping with the little legs, but

Giant Millipedes feel amazing to hold, but be very careful they cannot fall and hurt themselves by supporting them at all times.

make sure they are supported all the time and cannot fall. Rough handling of millipedes can make them produce a chemical from the sides of the body which stains the skin, so do be careful. This chemical is the millipede's defence; it tastes nasty and puts off predators such as birds. Millipedes are more likely to produce this chemical when you first start handling them, but they soon get used to being handled. Always wash your hands after handling any animal, but particularly

millipedes. Millipedes may also have little mites on their bodies, just like those on Hissing Cockroaches, and these normally do no harm.

It is possible to sex millipedes, but only some types are easy. Adult male Mombassan Train Millipedes have a shiny body and females are duller. In most other types of millipede both sexes look very similar, but the male is missing a pair of legs near to the head, on the 7th segment. When they mate, the male holds onto the

Observation Point

Movement

Millipedes have a huge number of legs, but manage to move very efficiently. You can watch your millipedes moving and measure how fast they move. As you watch a millipede walking, you can see the wave-like motion running up the body as each leg is moved forward in turn. Is each pair of legs working at the same time? How long does it take for the millipede to move all its legs forward, and does this vary with the speed it is moving? Put a millipede safely on a flat surface, and measure how long it takes for it to travel a certain distance, and how many times a wave motion goes up the body. You could also measure the footprints made by the millipede in a tray of damp sand. The footprints of ancient millipedes have been found as fossils from over 300 million years ago!

female and bends his head under hers. Look for millipedes mating to get a pair easily. The white eggs are laid singly in the soil, and are approximately 1-2mm (0.04-0.08in) long. Newly hatched millipedes are tiny and have fewer legs than the adults – they grow more segments as they get older. The young millipedes may be kept in with the adults, but look out for them, as they can hide amongst the food.

Giant Millipedes may take several years to reach maturity, depending upon the type of species. However, with the correct care they can easily be bred over several generations in captivity.

Nature's highly efficient recyclers, millipedes feed mainly on rotting vegetation or dead or decaying leaves. Fruit and vegetables will also be eaten.

Praying Mantis

Sphodromantis species

Arboreal

Insectivore

1 year

10cm (4in)

Sharp-eyed predators of the insect world, Praying Mantids can make very responsive pets. Over 2,000 species of Praying Mantis are known from many parts of the world, but most species live in warmer regions. There is a common European species, *Mantis religiosa*, which does not occur in Britain but has been introduced to the USA. Mantids are very efficient predators, and feed mainly on other insects, although the biggest species can tackle larger animals like lizards and even small mice. They catch their prey with their specially adapted front legs which, when held upright at the front of the body, make them look like they are praying – hence their common name. Mantids have an amazing head, and look very alien-like with their huge eyes. If you look even closer, you might also see the tiny ocelli or simple eyes they have between the antennae.

Mantids are normally purchased as half-grown

This young mantis will have long wings over the abdomen when adult.

nymphs, which should be active and inquisitive to show they are healthy. They live for about a year.

Mantids need to be in upright arboreal containers, at least 3 times the length of the mantis in height, so that they have room to shed their skin as they grow. A container 30 x 20 x 20cm (12 x 8 x 8in) is suitable for one adult, as they must be kept singly. If the enclosure is too big they may have difficulty finding and catching their food. The container should be sprayed with water at least once a day for the mantis to drink. They also need some

The mantid's large eyes look for any slight movements to find prey.

Praying Mantids are the famous sharp-eyed predators of the insect world, and they can be kept successfully at home.

The front legs are modified into strong, sharp arms for holding prey.

Young Praying Mantids are always alert and ready to catch food.

This adult praying mantis is being held correctly in the hand, but be aware they can jump! Try not to hold on to them too tightly because they are delicate.

they will sometimes try to jump, and the adults with wings can fly. Remember that most Praying Mantids should be kept on their own, as they are likely to see each other as food. Some types may be kept together, like the Dead-leaf Mantids, but even these do better singly. Normally the only time you will want to put them together is to try to breed them.

You can tell a female mantis even when young by counting the number of segments on the abdomen – she has only 6, but the male has 7 or 8. Mantids are only ready to breed when adult and they have grown their wings. Female mantids have a reputation for eating the male. Although he can often escape unharmed, he has to be very careful when he approaches her. After mating only once, the female can produce up to 9 batches of eggs. These are laid in a frothy mass called an ootheca, which hardens in the air to protect the eggs. They hatch after about a month, depending on temperature. Newly hatched mantids are miniature versions of the adults. They all emerge at once, sometimes several hundred from one ootheca. Baby mantids need tiny food like fruit flies or hatchling crickets, and will start feeding almost straight away.

humidity to moult properly, so there should be some damp tissue or moist soil in the bottom. Tropical mantids will need a heat mat but some species can be kept at room temperature.

The best food for mantids is smaller live insects, such as flies, grasshoppers or moths. You can catch them food from outside, or buy live food, but be careful that crickets do not attack your mantis when it is moulting.

You can let your mantis walk onto your hand, but it is best not to try to hold onto it as they are quite delicate. Be careful, as

Observation Point

Eyesight

Praying mantids are very efficient predators, which rely on eyesight to find their food. You can observe how sharp your mantids eyesight is, and test how well they can see.

Mantids will suddenly stare straight at their food when they see it. When your mantis is hungry (which is most of the time), put an item of food, such as a cricket, in a box a distance away, say 50cm (20in) – can it see the movement? Try moving the prey nearer or further away, and work out over what distance the mantis can see.

Can you make the mantis think something else is food? Try wiggling a small twig in the same way as a cricket moves, and see if your mantis is fooled!

When breeding, mantids lay a large foam egg case called an ootheca on a branch.

Hissing Cockroach

Gromphadorhina portentosa

Terrestrial

Vegetarian

3-4 years

10cm (4in)

Cockroaches are a very ancient group of insects, which evolved over 300 million years ago. Although most people recognise cockroaches as pests, only a few types infest houses and become a problem, like the American Cockroach (which is now found worldwide). Many species of cockroach are actually very useful, and eat old plant matter that other animals will not eat – they are the rubbish collectors of the animal world. There are over 3,500 species known so far. The Hissing Cockroach is one of the largest in the world, and comes from Madagascar. It has a shiny dark brown body and a darker shield-like plate over the head, with long antennae. Unlike many species this cockroach does not have wings when adult, so cannot fly. They are called Hissing Cockroaches as they make a loud hissing sound by pushing air out of the breathing holes on the side of the body, to frighten off predators.

Hissing Cockroaches can usually be bought as nymphs or adults from specialist pet shops or breeders. They can live a relatively long time for insects, 3 or 4 years being normal. Hissing Cockroaches sometimes come with little fast-moving mites that live on their bodies. These mites are not harmful, and actually help to keep the cockroach clean, but are not essential for their survival. They will only become a problem if the tank becomes dirty and they build up in numbers, and thorough cleaning will help to get rid of them.

SIMILAR SPECIES

Death's Head Cockroach
Blabberus cranifer

•

Burrowing Cockroach
Pycnoscelus surinamensis

•

American Cockroach
Periplaneta americana

Cockroaches will need a terrestrial container, with some pieces of bark or wood to climb on. Make sure the lid fits well to prevent them escaping, as they could climb the sides. They will need heating as they come from a warm climate. A group of up to 6 adults can be kept in a 30cm (12in) long tank, or more in a larger container. Give them plenty of hiding spaces. They are mainly nocturnal, so will be more active at night.

Hissing Cockroaches will eat most types of plant food. Offer them pieces of vegetables and fruit as their main food, and leaf litter can also be added for them to chew on. Cockroaches are mainly vegetarian, but as they are scavengers they will also take some fish flake or pellet food as well. Cockroaches may also be fed scraps of human food.

This type of cockroach can make a loud hissing sound from its abdomen.

Although many types have wings, Hissing Cockroaches do not and cannot fly.

Hissing Cockroaches are one of the largest cockroach species in the world.

Cockroaches are intelligent insects, and use their antennae to communicate with each other.

A giant cockroach may not appeal to everyone, but they can make great pets. They are useful creatures as they eat things that other animals leave behind.

Only the adult male Hissing Cockroach (on the left) has prominent horns on his head. Males use these horns to fight with each other.

Handling these big insects is not too difficult, but they can run quite fast. They also have some spines on their legs so be careful. They can be lifted out of the tank on a piece of wood, and then coaxed onto the hand. True to their name, they will hiss when they are disturbed, but soon become tame and hiss less often.

Breeding Hissing Cockroaches is possible if there are males and females present. Adult males have horns on the top of the thorax, females are smoother. Males use these horns to fight with each other. In the wild a male lives with a group of females, his 'harem', and defends his territory against other males, so it is a good idea to have no more than one adult male in the container. After mating, the female produces an egg case which is normally kept inside her body, although it is sometimes exposed at her rear end. The baby cockroaches emerge later and will stay close to their mother to begin with, before becoming independent. Young Hissing Cockroaches can be kept safely with adults, but make sure the container does not become too overcrowded.

Communication

Cockroaches generally are quite social creatures, and like other insects use their antennae for communication – almost like 'talking' to each other. They are actually closely related to termites, which form big social colonies much like ants. Their long antennae are used primarily to recognise other individuals, and you can see them regularly touching each other with them. Watch how much the antennae are used, particularly by the biggest male, checking on his group of females. If you separate an individual even just for a few hours, then reintroduce it, the other cockroaches will spend some time seeing who it is. How does a mother cockroach react to her babies?

Female Hissing Cockroaches are good mothers, and will look after their newborn young.

Land Hermit Crab

Coenobita clypeatus

Terrestrial

Omnivore

10-15 years

10cm (4in)

There are many different types of crabs in the world, and most of them are aquatic, particularly living in the sea. Land Hermit Crabs are adapted for living out of the water, and use an old shell from another animal, usually a mollusc, to form their own mobile home. The crab itself is pink or reddish-brown in colour, often with bluish claws. They walk around waving their antennae and dragging the shell behind them. In warmer climates, Land Hermit Crabs can occur in large numbers on tropical beaches.

Hermit crabs can be purchased from a dealer. They are sold usually as juveniles of about 5-7cm (2-3in), or as young adults of 10cm (4in), but sometimes bigger specimens are available up to adult size, which can be more than 15cm (6in) depending on the type of shell they are living in, although they rarely get this big in captivity. They can live a very long time if well cared for, and have been

SIMILAR SPECIES

Blue Land Crab
Cardiosoma species

A hermit crab's legs are very strong, and they are remarkably good climbers.

The eyes of hermit crabs are very sensitive to movement.

Land Hermit crabs are long-lived, comical pets which are easy to care for. They are adapted to living on land and use an old shell to form their mobile home.

Hermit crabs use shells of other animals, particularly molluscs, as mobile homes.

The enlarged claws at the front are quite powerful, and could nip fingers.

known to survive for over 10 years.

A terrestrial tank is needed for hermit crabs, but sand is better than a soil substrate, ideally washed silver sand. Keep this damp in places, to give the crabs areas to bury themselves to moult. Pebbles, rocks and driftwood can be added to give the crabs things to climb over in their search for food. Any plants will normally be destroyed by the crabs, so are better left out. They like a large, open water bowl that they can climb into, like a ceramic dog bowl – but there must be pieces of wood or bark leading in and out of it to prevent them drowning.

Hermit crabs require heating to create a tropical atmosphere. A group of 2 or 3 juvenile crabs can be kept in a 30cm (12in) long tank. Crabs of different sizes may fight if kept together.

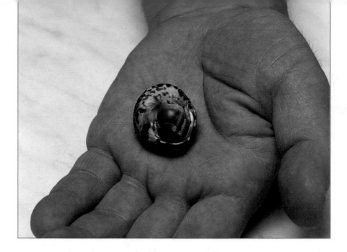

When first disturbed, Land Hermit Crabs will hide in their shell, but they soon become active again.

Land Hermit Crabs are quite active animals, and are scavengers, feeding on a wide range of plant and animal matter. They can be fed an omnivore diet, including a mixture of vegetables and fruit, with some dog or cat food or dead insects. They will also eat fish flake, and particularly like pellet food soaked in water. Foods can be given in a shallow dish to make cleaning any uneaten food easier. Land Hermit Crabs should always have some cuttlefish bone available in the tank, as they will actively eat this to help them moult successfully.

The most difficult thing about keeping hermit crabs is getting them to moult successfully, and providing enough of the right sized shells. Land Hermit Crabs will shed their exoskeleton at regular intervals to grow. They will usually hide away under a piece of wood or stone in a damper part of the tank when moulting, so should not be disturbed. When they grow in size, they may use their old shell for a while but will

be looking for a larger home, so like to have a selection of shells to choose from. Try to give them a good variety of shells in the container. Shells can be purchased, or collected from the seashore.

Handling hermit crabs is easy, but remember if they feel insecure they may try to hold on with their claws – which can be very strong and painful. Lift them up gently by the shell and place them in your hand, where they can then start to move around on their own. Be careful not to let them drop on the floor, and it is a good idea to handle them over a table or near the ground so they cannot fall far.

Land Hermit Crabs cannot be bred in captivity. In the wild they will lay their eggs in the sea, where they hatch and live as free-swimming larvae before eventually coming on land. Land Hermit Crabs are very common, so luckily do not need to be bred for pets.

Observation Point

Shell Choice

Land Hermit Crabs are very inquisitive, and particularly like investigating old mollusc shells. They are always looking for potential new homes, so you can observe what kind of shells they like. A tank of Land Hermit Crabs should normally have a selection of shells in it, for the crabs to choose from. To study what shells they prefer, take all the spare shells out for several days, then put some of them back. Try putting in groups of shells of different sizes – the crabs will normally be interested in them, and start looking over the shells, even dragging them a little to see how heavy they are. The shape and weight of the shell are important to the crab, as both affect how easy it is to carry around. Do they like conical, pointed shells, or prefer more rounded ones? The shells shown below are not suitable, so a hermit crab would search elsewhere for one that was more to its liking.

When a crab has selected a shell it likes, it is amazing how quickly it slips out of the old one and into the new.

Mealworm Beetle

Tenebrio molitor

Terrestrial

Vegetarian

3-4 months

2cm (0.75in)

Beetles are the biggest group of animals on the planet, with over 300,000 species known. However, many of them are difficult to keep and breed at home. Mealworm Beetles are, however, very easy to keep and breed very well. Although they are often only kept as food for birds or reptiles, mealworms can make interesting pets in their own right. The golden brown, burrowing larvae are the young of the adult beetles, which are black. The beetles are very active and climb a lot but do not fly much.

Mealworm Beetles can be purchased as larvae (the mealworm) from petshops or live-food dealers. The larvae take several weeks before they grow to adults, depending on the temperature, and the adult beetles live about a couple of months.

A terrestrial container is suitable for Mealworm Beetles, and they are happy at room temperature. They can be kept on

The hard wing cases on the beetle's back are called the elytra.

Mealworm Beetles are often very active, crawling around looking for food.

The pair of antennae on the head are the main sense organs.

a 8-10cm (3-4in) depth of quite dry soil, but also do just as well on dry bran flakes, which you can buy from a health food shop. The larvae will crawl around in the substrate, with the adult beetles staying on the surface and climbing on bark or other bits of wood. They could be kept in underground type accommodation (like a formicarium) where the burrows of the larvae may be seen. Make sure that the lid is secure to prevent escapes.

Mealworms are mainly vegetarian, and will feed on any type of vegetable or fruit. Slice pieces of food and place them on the surface of the substrate where both adults and larvae can reach them. Be careful to remove any food items before they start to go off, making sure that small larvae are not thrown away accidentally.

These insects are called mealworms because they will eat dry foods like corn meal and pellet foods, so these can be fed to them as well. They will

A colony of mealworms is a hive of activity, centred around eating!

Mealworms often end up as food for other creatures, but they are interesting pets themselves. They are very active and easy to breed.

The golden coloured beetle larva, the mealworm, usually burrows around within the substrate. It grows quickly and moults into a pupa.

also feed on the wood in the container, and particularly like chewing their way through cork bark.

Mealworms will breed freely in the container. The adults mate and lay their eggs on the ground. The eggs are very small and you are unlikely to see them. Newly hatched larvae are tiny, like very small worms, and grow quickly to become 2cm (0.75in) in length, before moulting into a white, maggot-like stage called a pupa, usually in the substrate or under a piece of bark. This is a resting stage, before they turn into the adult beetle, which is pale at first before darkening over a few hours to the normal black colour. It is fascinating to watch the amazing transformation from larva to adult.

SIMILAR SPECIES

Giant Mealworm
Zoophobas morio

•

Rhinoceros Beetle
Oryctes species *or Xylotrupes* species

•

Fruit Beetle
Pachnoda species

Black Garden Ant

Lasius niger

Underground

Omnivore

1-2 years

4mm (0.15in)

In sheer numbers of individuals, ants are some of the most abundant creatures on earth. They are fascinating social insects that form colonies with one or more queens controlling a group of workers. Ants can be kept indoors in a special container called a formicarium, where their burrows can be seen.

Ant nests can be dug up on private land, such as a garden or in a field where you have the owner's consent. Sometimes companies that supply the container will also supply live ants. Choose a small nest of ants. It is usually easy to see where they are by following some workers to the underground nest. The easiest way is to collect a group of ants from under a loose paving stone. Collect the white grub-like larvae and pupae (sometimes called 'ant eggs') as well as the adult workers, and try to collect a queen, who will be bigger than the worker ants. An ant colony can survive for 1-2 years in captivity, depending on whether queens are present.

The formicarium should have a shallow layer of soil put in at the bottom, with some spare soil kept ready to add afterwards. It may be easiest to take the container to where the ants are. Dig up the ants and transfer the soil with the nest of ants into the formicarium, poured in from the top.

SIMILAR SPECIES

Yellow Meadow Ant
Lasius flavus

Add a bit more soil up to 2-3cm (1in) from the top, and then put the cover on. Any stray ants can be put in carefully through the smaller access door. Do not worry about the jumble of soil, larvae and ants – it is amazing how quickly they set about tidying up the nest, and creating their tunnels. It is a good idea to cover over the sides of the container with some dark card, at least to begin with, because this will make the ants feel more secure creating their burrows.

Ants should be fed an omnivore diet, with sugar water or honey an important supplement. Another dish for drinking water should also be given. Foods include mixed vegetables, fruit, dead insects, dog or cat food, fish flake or pellets; in fact you can try them on just about anything. Add small pieces at first, to gauge how much they want to eat.

The ant colony consists mainly of sterile female workers, which do not lay eggs. As long as you have at least one queen in your ant nest, she will produce more worker ants. It is not possible actually to mate ants in captivity, as they need to fly to do so.

Individual ants 'talk' to each other using their antennae.

All the ants on these pages are workers – the queen is much fatter.

Like all insects, ants have three pairs of legs connected to the thorax.

Worker ants create a maze of tunnels underground, to form their nest.

A colony of Black Garden Ants, busy building their nest, will make a great exhibit. Each colony has one or more queens controlling a group of workers.

Chilean Rose Spider

Grammostola spatulata

Terrestrial

Insectivore

15 years

15cm (6in)

There are over 34,000 species of spiders, and around 700 are in the family Theraphosidae, variously called bird-eating spiders, mygales or 'tarantulas'. This group includes the biggest spiders in the world, which can grow up to 25cm (10in) leg span. The Chilean Rose is a popular pet species, reaching 15cm (6in), with a pale brown body and some attractive rosy-red hairs.

Spiders can be purchased from a dealer or pet shop, but try to get one that has been captive bred, not just caught from the wild. One of the best sources is through a spider group or society, where people have captive-bred spiders for sale, and can also give advice on keeping them. Spiders will normally be supplied newly hatched (called spiderlings) or as juveniles, which will quickly grow and live a long time – adult spiders will be of uncertain age and could be carrying diseases.

Long hairs on the legs help the spider detect movement around them.

The Chilean Rose is the most commonly available species of large spider.

The mouth is hidden between 2 pedipalps at the front of the body.

Newly hatched Chilean Rose spiderlings take around 1-2 years to reach adult size, and could then live a further 10 years or more – so are a long-term pet.

A terrestrial container is suitable for a large Chilean Rose Spider. They must be

The large abdomen carries some irritating hairs, normally used only in defence.

Spiders like this Chilean Rose are a popular choice, but must be looked after properly. It is best not to handle them since they are delicate and they can also bite.

kept on their own or they will fight. A 2-3cm (1in) layer of damp peat or compost is suitable as a substrate, or use vermiculite (a sterile material used for plants) which stays clean for longer. Spiderlings need to be kept in smaller containers such as round plastic pots 3cm (1.2in) wide and 3cm (1.2in) high, covered by well-fitting lids with ventilation. The base can be covered with about 5mm (0.2in) of peat or vermiculite, kept damp. Spiders must have drinking water in a dish or, when small, a ball of soaked cotton wool. All bird-eating spiders are tropical, and need to be kept warm. Use a heat mat connected to a thermostat. Smaller containers can be kept in a larger tank or box which is heated.

Spiders are predators, and need an insectivorous diet. Spiderlings should be fed very small crickets a couple of times a week, whereas adult spiders will take adult crickets or locusts and should be offered food once every couple of weeks. They are called bird-eating spiders as in the wild some species have even been known to catch small birds. These spiders can go for long

SIMILAR SPECIES

Curly-haired Spider
Brachypelma albopilosa

•

Red-knee Spider
Brachypelma smithi

In a tank like this, 2 spiders can be kept side by side provided they are separated from each other with a suitable divider.

periods without food, so do not be concerned if they do not feed for several weeks, as long as they look healthy. They will also stop feeding before they are going to moult, and will not resume feeding for a week or two afterwards. Going off their food is a sign that the spider may want to moult. It is important that live food is removed if the spider does not want to eat, as they can be annoyed by insects being present, and a cricket could damage a moulting spider.

It is not recommended to handle spiders at home. Firstly they are very delicate, and can be easily damaged if they fall. The abdomen could burst open if the spider is dropped even a small distance. Secondly they are capable of biting, although the bite is normally no worse than a bee sting. Also species from the New World like the Chilean Rose can flick hair from the rear of the abdomen, which can cause an irritation to the skin like nettle rash, and is even worse if the hairs get into your throat or eyes. If it is necessary to move a spider, you can transfer it by coaxing it into a smaller container with a piece of card or a ruler, without having to touch the spider at all.

Breeding spiders is not easy. Male spiders do not live very long, which is why females make better pets. Mating the spiders can be a tricky business, best left to someone with experience, so again contact with a spider keeper society is worthwhile. The female often tries to eat the male if he is not careful. If a pairing is successful, after a month or so the female will produce an egg sac made of silk, which will take a further month to hatch. Several hundred babies could emerge, which will need to be kept separately.

Observation Point

Growth and Development

It is amazing to see how arthropods change their exoskeleton to grow, and you have a good chance of observing this with spiders. Just before moulting, the big bird-eating spiders lay down a layer of silk on the ground, then turn onto their back. This is normal, and it is important they are not disturbed. Usually this happens at night, but if you are lucky you will see them doing it during the day. The spider pushes the old exoskeleton above its body, leaving what looks like another dead spider beside itself. The freshly moulted spider rests for a while, before flipping itself the right way up. When the spider has recovered, you can remove the old exoskeleton. Bird-eating spiders can get a bald patch at the rear of the abdomen, where they have lost some of the irritating hairs. This patch turns black just before moulting, and all the hairs will be replaced on the fresh exoskeleton. If you have a young spider, keep notes on when it moults, and take measurements from the old skin. The exoskeletons can be set out in a lifelike position when damp, and you could set up a display to make a permanent record of your spider's growth.

American Moon Moth

Actias luna

Arboreal

Vegetarian

3-4 months

12cm (5in)

Butterflies and moths (Lepidoptera) are often considered the most popular insects. The brilliant colours of butterflies can overshadow the generally duller moths, but some moths rival them in beauty, in particular the silkmoths. These often have spectacular markings and strikingly shaped wings, and the caterpillars can be equally bizarre. Moon moths have bright yellow-green wings with purple and white markings, and long tails on the rear wings. The plump green larvae or caterpillars are also interesting, with spines and hairs over the body.

Silkmoths can be ordered through the post from Lepidoptera supply companies, or are often sold at special entomological shows that take place on a regular

Wing markings and colour are important in identifying moths.

American Moon Moths live only for a short period of time as an adult, but live longer at the larval stage.

basis throughout the country. They can be purchased as eggs or cocoons, or sometimes as young larvae.

Eggs of silkmoths should be kept in a small clear plastic box until the larvae start to emerge, which usually takes about 2 weeks. Keep the young larvae in a box about 15 x 10cm (6 x 4in) with paper towelling or tissue on the base, and add a few leaves. A small box is good as the larvae are near the food at all times. An arboreal container is suitable for rearing the larvae when they have grown over 1cm (0.5in) in length. Then they can be kept on cut foliage in water. The container must be cleaned regularly, to prevent disease. Overcrowding can cause problems as well, so if you have many larvae, separate them into a few containers. The caterpillars take about 6 weeks to grow, but development time varies, being quicker at higher temperatures. Once they reach full size, about 4cm (1.5in) in length,

The feathery antennae are used by males to find their mate.

The beautiful adult Moon Moth only lives a few weeks, and does not feed.

Both male and female moths have long tails on the hind wings.

SIMILAR SPECIES

Indian Moon Moth
Actias selene

•

Robin Moth
Hyalophora cecropia

•

Emperor Moth
Saturnia pavonia

These 2 objects are the cocoons of American Moon Moths, spun from silk by the larvae.

they will start to spin a protective covering for their pupa out of silk, called a cocoon. This is made either on the ground or in amongst the leaves or branches. When finished, the cocoons can be collected up, cutting the branches if necessary or very carefully peeling the silk away from the side of the container. They should then be transferred to the base of a hanging net before emergence as moths. The pupae are a resting stage, and it can be several weeks before the moths emerge. The net cage is very important to stop the adult moths damaging themselves too much when they fly.

American Moon Moth caterpillars feed mainly on walnut or birch leaves, but will also eat leaves from other trees including oak, elm, willow, hazel, or cherry. Once started on one type of leaf, it is best to keep them on the same type throughout their development. Caterpillars are like

Observation Point

Eating

Caterpillars are terrific consumers of food. Unlike adult silkmoths, which have no mouthparts and cannot eat, their caterpillars are little more than eating machines. The amount they eat is surprising, and you can work out just how much in weight of food your caterpillars eat over a period of time. Using a good kitchen scale, weigh the leaves (including the branches) before you feed the caterpillars. Add the food to the caterpillars, then, when all the leaves have been eaten, weigh the branches that are left and take this away from the original figure to get the weight of leaves eaten. To compare this to the weight of the caterpillars, you can weigh them using the same method, by carefully removing them from the plants.

Some of these caterpillars will eat several times their own weight in food per day!

eating machines, and you will be amazed how quickly they chew through the leaves, so make sure they are kept supplied with food. The adults, however, do not feed. They have no mouthparts, and store up enough energy as larvae to survive the short time it takes to find a mate and breed.

It is better not to touch the delicate larvae. Newly hatched caterpillars can be transferred by using a small paint brush to scoop them off of the side of a box, and larger larvae can be moved to new foliage by placing their old branches at the base of the fresh food, and letting them transfer themselves. Adult moths can be persuaded to hold onto your hand, but be warned – they will often go to the toilet on you when they first emerge! Do not forget that they are also good fliers, so make sure the windows are closed if you have let them out.

Adult male moon moths are smaller bodied than females, with longer tails on the wings. Also males have larger, more feather-like antennae. Male silkmoths use their antennae to find females, and some species can smell them from more than 1km (0.6 miles) away. Moon moths should mate readily if there are both sexes present in a net cage.

The female will then lay 100-200 eggs on the side of the net, where they can be collected up after a few days. The adult moths die naturally soon after mating and egg-laying. In the wild, American Moon Moths breed twice in the year, the second brood overwintering as pupae, with the new moths emerging in the spring. In captivity the pupae can be kept in the fridge, then warmed up when there are leaves for the next generation of larvae to feed on.

A group of part-grown American Moon Moth larvae, feeding on birch leaves. They are like eating machines and will chew through the leaves very quickly.

Leaf Insect

Phyllium bioculatum

Arboreal

Vegetarian

6-8 months

8cm (3in)

Leaf Insects are closely related to stick insects, but have even more amazing camouflage, and look just like the leaves they feed on. They are found in Asia, and different types can be between 8 and 16cm (3 and 6.5in) long. The most common species in captivity is *Phyllium bioculatum*, from Sri Lanka, one of the smaller types.

Leaf Insects are usually only available as eggs, although sometimes nymphs are offered for sale. It is best to get experience of keeping and breeding different types of stick insects before trying to keep Leaf Insects. Once they hatch, Leaf Insects only live for 6 months or so.

A container set up as for stick insects will be suitable for Leaf Insects. They must have heating, such as a heat mat on the side of the container to warm it to 21-25°C (70-77°F). Humidity is very important. Spray your pets with a fine mist several times a day to

SIMILAR SPECIES

Giant Leaf Insect
Phyllium giganteum

Adult Leaf Insects have wings folded over the back of the body.

Every part of the insect is camouflaged to look like leaves, even the legs.

Leaf Insects sway from side to side when walking, like leaves in the wind.

The large, leaf-shaped abdomen is easily visible in this large nymph.

keep them damp and give them drinking water. It is best to have peat at the bottom of the container to help keep up the humidity. This should be replaced regularly, remembering to look for eggs if adults are kept.

Leaf Insects feed on leaves and in captivity they are usually fed on bramble or oak leaves. Find out what your insects were being fed on before you get them. It is most important that the leaves given to the Leaf Insects are really fresh, to keep the animals healthy. You may handle your Leaf Insects, but be careful as they are delicate.

Breeding Leaf Insects is not easy, as even if they lay eggs these do not always hatch. They can breed without males, but the chances of success are better if males (which are smaller, with wings) are present with females. If you are lucky and they do breed, eggs will be dropped singly on the bottom of the container. They are an odd shape, with ridges along the side, and are camouflaged to look like caterpillar droppings. They should be collected and kept warm in a box on damp sand or soil until they hatch. Newly emerged Leaf Insects are pinky-red in colour, and are miniature versions of the adults. They must be carefully looked after and do best if they are kept with some small stick insects, which encourage them to feed by chewing the leaves. They take 4-5 months to grow to adult size.

Almost impossible to spot in the wild, these Leaf Insects are masters of camouflage. They are found in forests and look like the leaves they feed on.

Imperial Scorpion

Pandinus imperator

Terrestrial

Insectivore

7 years

16cm (6.5in)

Scorpions are arachnids, in the same group as the spiders. They are one of the most feared invertebrate creatures, due to their reputation for carrying powerful stings. But the largest species can rely on their size and strength, so do not always have a nasty venom. The Imperial Scorpion is one of these, and can make a spectacular pet, but must be given the right conditions to thrive.

Imperial Scorpions can be acquired from some pet shops or animal dealers. They are now protected from over-collection in the wild, so can only be imported under licence. Try to get captive-bred scorpions, as more people are having success in rearing young scorpions. This large black species will reach an impressive 16cm (6.5in) or more, and can live up to 7 years.

Terrestrial accommodation is suitable for scorpions, and they require the same conditions as the large spiders, namely a tropical, humid environment, with a heat mat connected to a thermostat. These scorpions like to dig, so can be given a deeper substrate of damp soil to let them burrow naturally, and several pieces of bark or large flat rocks for extra hiding places. Unlike spiders, several Imperial Scorpions can be kept together, although there may be some fighting. Two or 3 adults can be kept in a 60cm (24in) long tank. Scorpions are normally nocturnal, so use a red light to see them active in the dark.

Scorpions are insectivores, and can be fed mainly crickets and locusts. Young scorpions can be given dead insects, and will eat

SIMILAR SPECIES

Jungle Scorpion
Heterometrus species

•

Yellow Scorpion
Scorpio maurus

Imperial Scorpions are nocturnal, and become much more active at night.

The scorpion's sting is held at the rear end of the body.

Although no worse than a bee sting, it is best to avoid being stung!

The claws are very large and powerful.

things like mealworms with relish. Adults will also sometimes eat dead food. They will only need to be offered food once or twice a week, and you should remove any uneaten food with tweezers.

Do not handle Imperial Scorpions, even though they are not normally dangerous. The sting is usually only equivalent to that of a bee but is still better avoided. They also have very strong claws, which can give a very painful nip. Big specimens have been known to break pencils with their claws, so imagine what they could do to your finger!

Breeding scorpions is possible at home, but is not always successful. With a group of adults, there is a chance you have a pair, but it is difficult to sex them. Look out for any that are unusually fat, which may be

Imperial Scorpions are impressive animals, that must be treated with respect in captivity. Do not handle them, even though they are not normally dangerous.

pregnant, and separate them from the others if possible. If you are lucky, you may get a female with a group of glistening white babies. There can be between 20 and 50 born, which climb up onto her back and stay there for 3-4 weeks. During this period she should be left undisturbed or she will eat her young. When they moult and come off the female's back they can be separated from their mother, and reared separately in the same way as the adults. They will take several years to grow to adulthood.

Apple Snail

Pomacea palludosa

Aquatic

Vegetarian

2-3 years

8cm (3in)

Apple Snails are aquatic molluscs, one of the largest groups of invertebrates. They are one of the few large molluscs that can be kept easily at home, and are quite entertaining. Snails might not immediately seem a good choice as a pet, but can be very rewarding and Apple Snails are certainly different.

Aquarium shops often have Apple Snails for sale. Make sure you buy healthy-looking snails, that are active and feeding. They may live several years, and grow to apple-sized proportions of up to 8cm (3in), hence the name.

SIMILAR SPECIES

Common Pond Snail
Limnea stagnates

•

Great Ram's-horn Snail
Planorbarius corneus

When disturbed, Apple Snails use their shell to protect their soft bodies.

An aquatic tank is needed to keep Apple Snails. An aquarium 30 x 20 x 20cm (12 x 8 x 8in) would be enough for only 2 or 3 adults, so if you want to breed them, a tank at least 60cm (24in) long by 30cm (12in) high is recommended. Then a group of adults and young can be kept. They like water to a depth of only about 10cm (4in), so do not fill the tank to the top with water. Apple Snails lay their eggs above the surface, so the height above the water is necessary. Add some branches or pieces of wood above the water line for the snails to climb. They will walk up even the vertical sides of the tank, so a lid is necessary. A heater-thermostat is needed to keep the water at a temperature of 25°C (77°F), and an internal filter is best for keeping the water clean. A large number of Apple Snails can be quite dirty, so needs regular water changes. Having a good light above the tank is worthwhile, both for seeing the snails and for encouraging algae, which the snails will eat.

Apple Snails are vegetarians, feeding mainly on leafy vegetables. Cabbage is a favourite, and they can also be fed lettuce. Also try them on various types of root vegetables or fruit, but only feed them small amounts at a time, so that it does not foul the water. They will also eat fish

Apple Snails get their common name from the large, rounded shell.

The huge freshwater Apple Snail, measuring up to 8cm (3in) as an adult, makes a very active and rather unusual aquatic pet.

The long tentacles at the front of the body act like antennae in insects.

The snail's eyes are at the base of the tentacles in aquatic snails.

flake and pellet foods. Calcium is a vital additive, for the formation of the shells. Keep a whole piece of cuttlefish bone in the water for the snails to rasp on, and replace it when all the soft white calcium has been eaten. They also eat green algae that grows on the sides of the tank. You can add aquatic plants for them to eat, or green algae-covered rocks from a pond or stream.

To breed Apple Snails, you will need several adults to guarantee having animals of both sexes. Unlike many snails which are hermaphrodite, meaning they are both male and female at the same time, Apple Snails are one or the other – but there is no way of telling by looking at them. If you have fertile females, they will start laying eggs in batches of 20-100, above the water. Sometimes these can be over 30cm (12in) above the water line. The foul-tasting eggs are bright coral-pink in colour, to dissuade other animals from eating them. After a week or two, the eggs hatch and the baby snails fall back into the water. They are tiny versions of the adults, with their own little shells, and start to feed like the adults straight away.

Apple Snails are often sold in aquarium

Apple Snails have voracious appetites, and can consume large amounts of leaves like cabbage and lettuce. They can also eat root vegetables and fruit.

shops not just because they are an unusual addition to a fish tank. They are valuable because they encourage infusoria, a kind of freshwater plankton that is good food for baby fish.

It is just as interesting to keep land snails as aquatic snails. Many different species can be kept in terrestrial accommodation, and fed a vegetarian diet. Just like the Apple Snails, they will need a calcium supplement such as cuttlefish bone for them to rasp on. Most species will not need heating, but tropical snails will need a heat source to keep them active. They also like high humidity, and if it is too dry and/or humid, they will seal themselves in their shells until conditions get better. Common garden snails like *Helix aspersa* or *Cepea* species can be kept, or tropical species like the huge Giant African Land Snail *Achatina fulica*.

Close up, you can see the growth rings on the shell of an Apple Snail. Calcium is a vital additive for the formation of snail shells.

Observation Point

Breathing

Apple Snails have a really obvious breathing tube, which sticks out on one side of the body. Unlike some animals which have gills, and can breathe underwater, Apple Snails have to come to the surface to breathe. Rather than coming right out of the water, they extend the breathing tube to the surface, and use it like a snorkel to take in air.

You can see how often they need to collect air through the breathing tube, and how long they can go before breathing again. Is there any difference when the snails are more active, or when they are fed? Does the temperature of the water affect them too?

Record Card

It is a good idea to have a record card for each type of animal you keep, so that you can make a note of important events such as moults or breeding. You can also make a note of feeding behaviour, and anything to do with a study that you may carry out on your pets including the suggested projects in this book.

You can look back on your records to check how old your animals are, and what foods they like. Some can be difficult to breed, and records of each animal and when they became adult is useful before attempted matings. Eggs take some time to develop, and details of the date laid and temperature will indicate when they are due to hatch. Records are also vital if your animals ever become sick. You will need information on what happened and when, before getting some advice from a veterinarian or other expert.

Good zoos keep detailed records of all the animals in their care, which they share with other collections. This is particularly important in conservation programmes for threatened species, which may rely upon captive breeding for their survival. Although none of the invertebrates in this book are endangered, you should create the best possible conditions for your pets, and good record keeping will help. You could also share information with other pet-keepers in the Societies listed in the 'useful information' section (p.63).

Record Card

Species _____   Temperature _____

Name _____   Humidity _____

Number of arrivals _____   Preferred foods _____

Arrival date _____   _____

Date	Event	Notes
e.g. for a spider		
23 June	Moult	*Started moulting at 6 o'clock, seems to be OK.*
		Left undisturbed
24 June		*Looking fine, much bigger now.*
30 June	Fed	*Tried with a cricket, eaten straight away.*

Creepy Crawly Quiz

How well do you now know your invertebrates?

The answers to the following quiz are all in the previous pages.

1. Name 2 types of foodplant for the Indian Stick Insect.

2. What is the egg case of a mantid called?

3. How do Hissing Cockroaches hiss?

4. What kind of shells do Land Hermit Crabs usually live in?

5. How many species of beetle are there in the world?

6. What is a container designed for keeping ants called?

7. How do you tell the difference between a centipede and a millipede?

8. What do bird-eating or tarantula spiders do when they shed their exoskeleton?

9. How do male Moon moths find a mate?

10. How many babies could an Imperial Scorpion give birth to?

11. What colour are Apple Snail eggs?

Answers

1. Privet, ivy or bramble. 2. An ootheca. 3. By pushing air out of their breathing holes. 4. Mollusc or snail shells. 5. Over 300,000 species. 6. A formicarium. 7. Millipedes have 2 pairs of legs per segment, whereas centipedes have 1 pair. 8. Lay silk onto the ground, and then flip over onto their backs. 9. The male uses his antennae to smell her, sometimes over 1km (0.6 miles) away. 10. 20-50. 11. Bright pink.